LEADER'S GUIDE

UNLOCKING DESTINIES
FROM THE
COURTS OF
HEAVEN

UNLOCKING DESTINIES
FROM THE
COURTS OF
HEAVEN

DISSOLVING CURSES THAT
DELAY AND DENY OUR FUTURES

ROBERT
HENDERSON

DESTINY IMAGE® PUBLISHERS, INC.

P.O. Box 310, Shippensburg, PA 17257-0310

"Promoting Inspired Lives."

This book and all other Destiny Image and Destiny Image Fiction books are available at Christian bookstores and distributors worldwide.

Cover design by Eileen Rockwell
Interior design by Terry Clifton

For more information on foreign distributors, call 717-532-3040.

Reach us on the Internet: www.destinyimage.com.

ISBN 13 TP: 978-0-7684-1379-3

For Worldwide Distribution, Printed in the U.S.A.

8 9 10 11 12 / 23 22 21 20 19

CONTENTS

Introduction...7

Basic Leader Guidelines 9

Steps to Launching an Unlocking Destinies
From the Courts of Heaven Group or Class.....................13

Leader Checklist 16

Session Discussion Questions
Weekly Overview of Meetings/Group Sessions 18

SESSION 1   Three Dimensions of Prayer: Father, Friend, and Judge 23

SESSION 2   Operating in the Courts of Heaven 35

SESSION 3   Your Book of Destiny in Heaven 43

SESSION 4   What's Written in Your Book of Destiny? 55

SESSION 5   Retrieving and Unlocking Your Book.....................................61

SESSION 6   An Introduction to Curses 71

SESSION 7   Common Landing Places for Curses: Part 1..............................81

SESSION 8   Common Landing Places for Curses: Part 2..............................91

SESSION 9   Unlocking Your Prophetic Senses in the Courts of Heaven................103

INTRODUCTION

This guide is designed to practically equip group leaders to walk participants through the *Unlocking Destinies from the Courts of Heaven* course. This curriculum can be used as an individual study, or can be experienced in either a small group or church class setting. The objective for participants in simple: identify and dissolve the delaying forces that prevent them from discovering and walking in the fullness of their destinies. The most common delaying, hindering force aimed at destiny is a curse.

The following introduction is included at the beginning of each interactive manual. For each participant to successfully work through the curriculum, he or she will need to purchase a copy of the interactive manual, which reinforces the teaching presented on the video sessions.

INTRODUCTION
(FOR PARTICIPANTS)

The desire to see your destiny fulfilled is not a selfish ambition. When the body of Christ starts to see personal destinies fulfilled, by default, the powers of darkness will be pushed back and restrained in the earth. The devil's agenda for individuals, families, regions, and nations will be broken as you step into the assignments God has marked for your life—even before the foundation of the earth.

Throughout this course, you will recognize and confront different hindrances to you walking in the fullness of your destiny. It all begins with approaching God the Judge in the courts of Heaven. Remember, He wants to render judgments on *your* behalf. The key is coming with humility into the courts of Heaven and learning how to navigate this supernatural dimension of prayer.

You can approach this course as follows:

1.   You will learn how to interact with God the Judge through courtroom prayer.

2.   You will receive a basic understanding of how to operate in the courts of Heaven.

3.   You will discover what the books of Heaven or books of destiny are and why they are vital to you fulfilling your purpose.

4. You will evaluate the status of your own destiny: do you have a sense of destiny, but it remains elusive? Do you have no sense of destiny or purpose at all?

5. You will retrieve your book of destiny in Heaven, if it has been sold out.

6. You will open your book of destiny once it has been retrieved.

7. When you have access to your book of destiny, you will be able to have clarity on your purpose and also present cases before the courts of Heaven based on what's written in your book.

8. You will identify several common landing places that have given the devil legal right to plant curses in your life.

9. You will specifically renounce these landing places of legal right and repent for them, cancelling the curses from continuing in your life and in the lives of future generations.

10. You will ask the Lord to give you prophetic sight so that you can begin to discern how the spirit realm operates and thereby freely have access to what is written in the books of destiny in Heaven.

The end goal is:

- Providing you a supernatural prayer strategy where you can begin to prophetically see what is recorded in your unique book of destiny in Heaven.

- Pray these realities into being over your life and family.

- Discern and pray forth what is written in the books of other people, regions, cities, and even nations, as the Holy Spirit reveals.

Basic Leader Guidelines

This breakthrough study is designed to help you discover what you have been created for, legally deal with the works of the enemy that try to delay and deny your destiny, and break off any curse that has found legal right in your life or generational line.

There are several different ways that you can engage this study. By no means is this forthcoming list comprehensive. Rather, these are the standard outlets recommended to facilitate this curriculum. We encourage you to seek the Lord's direction, be creative, and prepare for supernatural transformation in your Christian life.

When all is said and done, this curriculum is unique in that the end goal is *not* information—it is transformation. The sessions are intentionally sequenced to take every believer on a journey from information, to revelation, to transformation.

Here are some of the ways you can use the curriculum:

1. Church Small Group

Often, churches feature a variety of different small group opportunities per season in terms of books, curriculum resources, and Bible studies. *Unlocking Destinies from the Courts of Heaven* would be included among the offering of titles for whatever season you are launching for the small group program.

It is recommended that you have at least four to five people to make up a small group and a maximum of twelve. If you end up with more than 12 members, either the group needs to multiply and break into two different groups or you should consider moving toward a church class model (which will be outlined below).

For a small group setting, here are the essentials:

- *Meeting place*: Either the leader's home or a space provided by the church.

- *Appropriate technology*: A DVD player attached to a TV that is large enough for all of the group members to see (and loud enough for everyone to hear).

- *Leader/Facilitator*: This person will often be the host, if the small group is being conducted at someone's home; but it can also be a team (husband/wife, two church leaders, etc.). The leader(s) will direct the session from beginning to end, from sending reminder e-mails to participating group members about the meetings, to closing out the sessions in prayer and dismissing everyone. That said, leaders might select certain people in the group to assist with various elements of the meeting—worship, prayer, ministry time, etc. A detailed description of what the group meetings should look like will follow in the pages to come.

SAMPLE SCHEDULE FOR HOME GROUP MEETING
(FOR A 7:00 P.M. MEETING)

- Before arrival: Ensure that refreshments are ready by 6:15 P.M. If they need to be refrigerated, ensure they are preserved appropriately until 15 minutes prior to the official meeting time.

- 6:15 P.M.: Leaders arrive at meeting home or facility.

- 6:15–6:25 P.M.: Connect with hosts, co-hosts, and/or co-leaders to review the evening's program.

- 6:25–6:35 P.M.: Pray with hosts, co-hosts, and/or co-leaders for the evening's events. Here are some sample prayer directives:

  - For the Holy Spirit to move and minister freely.

  - For the teaching to connect with and transform all who hear it.

  - For dialogue and conversation that edifies.

  - For comfort and transparency among group members.

  - For the Presence of God to manifest during worship.

  - For testimonies of answered prayers.

  - For increased hunger for God's Presence and power.

- 6:35–6:45: Ensure technology is functioning properly!

  - Test the DVDs featuring the teaching sessions, making sure they are set up to the appropriate session.

  - If you are doing praise and worship, ensure that either the MP3 player or CD player is functional, set at an appropriate volume (not soft, but not incredibly loud), and that song sheets are available for everyone so they can sing along with the lyrics. (If you are tech savvy, you could do a PowerPoint or Keynote presentation featuring the lyrics.)

- 6:45–7:00 P.M.: Welcome and greeting for guests.

- 7:00–7:10 P.M.: Fellowship, community, and refreshments.

- 7:10–7:12 P.M.: Gather everyone together in the meeting place.

- 7:12–7:30 P.M.: Introductory prayer and worship.

- 7:30–7:40 P.M.: Ministry and prayer time.

- 7:40–8:00 P.M.: Watch DVD session.

- 8:00–8:20 P.M.: Discuss DVD session.

- 8:20–8:35 P.M.: Activation time.

- 8:35–8:40 P.M.: Closing prayer and dismiss.

This sample schedule is *not* intended to lock you into a formula. It is simply provided as a template to help you get started. Our hope is that you customize it according to the unique needs of your group and sensitively navigate the activity of the Holy Spirit as He uses these sessions to supernaturally transform the lives of every person participating in the study.

2. SMALL GROUP CHURCH-WIDE CAMPAIGN

This would be the decision of the pastor or senior leadership of the church. In this model, the entire church would go through *Unlocking Destinies from the Courts of Heaven* in both the main services and ancillary small groups/life classes.

These campaigns would be marketed as *40 Days to Unlocking Destiny*. The pastor's weekend sermon would be based on the principles in *Unlocking Destinies from the Courts of Heaven*, and the Sunday school classes/life classes and/or small groups would also follow the *Unlocking Destinies from the Courts of Heaven* curriculum format.

3. CHURCH CLASS | MID-WEEK CLASS | SUNDAY SCHOOL CURRICULUM

Churches of all sizes offer a variety of classes purposed to develop members into more effective disciples of Jesus and agents of transformation in their spheres of influence.

Unlocking Destinies from the Courts of Heaven would be an invaluable addition to a church's class offering. Typically, churches offer a variety of topical classes targeted at men's needs, women's needs, marriage, family, finances, and various areas of Bible study.

Unlocking Destinies from the Courts of Heaven is a unique resource, as it does not fit in with the aforementioned traditional topics usually offered to the Church body. On the contrary, this study breaks down what it means to confront and overcome common factors that are responsible for delaying and denying destiny from being fulfilled.

While it may difficult to facilitate dialogue in a class setting, it is certainly optional and recommended. The other way to successfully engage *Unlocking Destinies from the Courts of Heaven* in a class setting is to have a teacher/leader go through the questions/answers presented in the upcoming pages and use these as his or her teaching notes.

4. INDIVIDUAL STUDY

While the curriculum is designed for use in a group setting, it also works as a tool that can equip anyone who is looking to strengthen his or her spirit and soul.

STEPS TO LAUNCHING AN UNLOCKING DESTINIES FROM THE COURTS OF HEAVEN GROUP OR CLASS

PREPARE WITH PRAYER!

Pray! If you are a **church leader**, prayerfully consider how *Unlocking Destinies from the Courts of Heaven* could transform the culture and climate of your church community!

If you are a **group leader** or **class facilitator**, pray for those who will be attending your group, signing up for your class, and will be positioning their lives to be transformed by the Power and Presence of God in this study.

PREPARE PRACTICALLY!

Determine how you will be using the Unlocking Destinies from the Courts of Heaven curriculum.

Identify which of the following formats you will be using the curriculum in:

- Church-sponsored small group study

- Church-wide campaign

- Church class (Wednesday night, Sunday morning, etc.)

- Individual study

Determine a meeting location and ensure availability of appropriate equipment.

Keep in mind the number of people who may attend. You will also need AV (audio-visual) equipment. The more comfortable the setting, the more people will enjoy being there, and will spend more time ministering to each other!

A word of caution here: the larger the group, the greater the need for co-leaders or assistants. The ideal small group size is difficult to judge; however, once you get more than 10 to 12 people, it becomes difficult for each member to feel "heard." If your group is larger than 12 people, consider either having two or more small group discussion leaders or "multiplying" the larger group into two smaller ones.

Determine the format for your meetings.

The Presence of the Lord, which brings transformation, is cradled and stewarded well in the midst of organization. Structure should never replace spontaneity; on the contrary, having a plan and determining what type of format your meetings will take enables you to flow with the Holy Spirit and minister more effectively.

Also, by determining what kind of meeting you will be hosting, you become well equipped to develop a schedule for the meeting, identify potential co-leaders, and order the appropriate number of resources.

Set a schedule for your meetings.

Once you have established the format for your meetings, set a schedule for your meetings. Some groups like to have a time of fellowship or socializing (either before or after the meeting begins) where light refreshments are offered. Some groups will want to incorporate times of worship and personal ministry into the small group or class. This is highly recommended for *Unlocking Destinies from the Courts of Heaven* as the study is designed to be founded upon equipping and activating believers through encountering God's Presence. The video portion and discussion questions are intended to instruct believers, while the worship, times of ministry, group interaction, prayer time, and activation elements are purposed to engage them to live out what they just learned. *Unlocking Destinies from the Courts of Heaven* is not a lofty theological concept; it is a practical reality for every born-again believer. This study is intended to educate; but even more so, it is designed to activate believers and position them to steward their private, interior lives.

Establish a start date along with a weekly meeting day and time.

This eight-week curriculum should be followed consistently and consecutively. Be mindful of the fact that while there are eight weeks of material, most groups will want to meet one last time after completing the last week to celebrate, or designate their first meeting as a time to get to know each other and "break the ice." This is very normal and should be encouraged to continue the community momentum that the small group experience initiates. Typically, after the final session is completed, groups will often engage in a social activity—either going out to dinner together, seeing a movie, or something of the like.

Look far enough ahead on the calendar to account for anything that might interfere. Choose a day that works well for the members of your group. For a church class, be sure to coordinate the time with the appropriate ministry leader.

Advertise!

Getting the word out in multiple ways is most effective. Print out flyers, post a sign-up sheet, make an announcement in church services or group meetings, send out weekly e-mails and text messages, set up your own blog or website, or post the event on the social media avenue you and your group utilize most (Facebook, Twitter, etc.). A personal invitation or phone call is a great way to reach those who might need that little bit of extra encouragement to get involved.

For any type of small group or class to succeed, it must be endorsed by and encouraged from the leadership. For larger churches with multiple group/class offerings, it is wise to provide church members literature featuring all of the different small group/class options. This information should also be displayed online in an easily accessible page on your church website.

For smaller churches, it is a good idea for the pastor or a key leader to announce the launch of a small group course or class from the pulpit during an announcement time.

Gather your materials.

Each leader will need the *Unlocking Destinies from the Courts of Heaven Leader's Kit*, as well as the *Unlocking Destinies from the Courts of Heaven* book.

Additionally, each participant will need a personal copy of the *Unlocking Destinies from the Courts of Heaven* interactive manual. It is recommended they also purchase the *Unlocking Destinies from the Courts of Heaven* book for further enrichment and as a resource to complement their daily readings. However, they are able to engage in the exercises and participate in the group discussion apart from reading the book.

We have found it best for the materials to all be purchased at one time—many booksellers and distributors offer discounts on multiple orders, and you are assured that each member will have their materials from the beginning of the course.

Step Forward!

Arrive at your meeting in *plenty* of time to prepare; frazzled last-minute preparations do not put you in a place of "rest," and your group members will sense your stress! Ensure that all AV equipment is working properly and that you have ample supplies for each member. Nametags are a great idea, at least for the first couple of meetings. Icebreaker and introduction activities are also a good idea for the first meeting.

Pray for your members. As much as possible, make yourself available to them. As members increase in insight on strengthening themselves in the Lord, they will want to share that discovery! You will also need to encourage those who struggle, grow weary, or lose heart along the journey and through the process. Make sure your members stay committed so they experience the full benefits of this teaching.

Embrace the journey that you and your fellow members are embarking on to strengthen themselves in the Lord. Transformation begins within *you*!

Multiply yourself. Is there someone you know who was not able to attend your group? Help them to initiate their own small group now that you know how effective hosting *Unlocking Destinies from the Courts of Heaven* can be in a group setting!

THANK YOU

Thank you for embarking on a journey to equip the people of God to see every hindering force broken off of their lives and step into new dimensions of purpose realized and destiny fulfilled.

LEADER CHECKLIST

ONE TO TWO MONTHS PRIOR

___ Have you determined a start date for your class or small group?

___ Have you determined the format, meeting day and time, and weekly meeting schedule?

___ Have you selected a meeting location (making sure you have adequate space and AV equipment available)?

___ Have you advertised? Do you have a sign-up sheet to ensure you order enough materials?

THREE WEEKS TO ONE MONTH PRIOR

___ Have you ordered materials? You will need a copy of *Unlocking Destinies from the Courts of Heaven* Leader's Kit, along with copies of the workbook and book for each participant.

___ Have you organized your meeting schedule/format?

ONE TO TWO WEEKS PRIOR

___ Have you received all your materials?

___ Have you reviewed the DVDs and your Leader's Guide to familiarize yourself with the material and to ensure everything is in order?

___ Have you planned and organized the refreshments, if you are planning to provide them? Some leaders will handle this themselves, and some find it easier to allow participants to sign up to provide refreshments if they would like to do so.

___ Have you advertised and promoted? This includes sending out emails to all participants, setting up a Facebook group, setting up a group through your church's database system (if available), promotion in the church bulletin, etc.

___ Have you appointed co-leaders to assist you with the various portions of the group/class? While it is not necessary, it is helpful to have someone who is in charge of either leading (on guitar, keyboard, etc.) or arranging the worship music (putting songs on a CD, creating song lyric sheets, etc.). It is also helpful to have a prayer coordinator as well—someone who helps facilitate the prayer time, ensuring that all of the prayer needs are acknowledged and remembered, and assigning the various requests to group members who are willing to lift up those needs in prayer.

FIRST MEETING DAY

___ Plan to arrive *early!* Give yourself extra time to set up the meeting space, double check all AV equipment, and organize your materials. It might be helpful to ask participants to arrive 15 minutes early for the first meeting to allow for distribution of materials and any icebreaker activity you might have planned.

SESSION DISCUSSION QUESTIONS WEEKLY OVERVIEW OF MEETINGS/ GROUP SESSIONS

Here are some instructions on how to use each of the weekly Discussion Question guides.

WELCOME AND FELLOWSHIP TIME
(10–15 MINUTES)

This usually begins five to ten minutes prior to the designated meeting time and typically continues up until ten minutes after the official starting time. Community is important. One of the issues in many small group/class environments is the lack of connectivity among the people. People walk around inspired and resourced, but they remain disconnected from other believers. Foster an environment where community is developed but, at the same time, not distracting. Distraction tends to be a problem that plagues small group settings more than classes.

Welcome: Greet everyone as they walk in. If it is a small group environment, as the host or leader, be intentional about connecting with each person as they enter the meeting space. If it is a church class environment, it is still recommended that the leader connect with each participant. However, there will be less pressure for the participants to feel connected immediately in a traditional class setting versus a more intimate small group environment.

Refreshments and materials: In the small group, you can serve refreshments and facilitate fellowship between group members. In a class setting, talk with the attendees and ensure that they purchase all of their necessary materials (workbook and optional copy of *Unlocking Destinies from the Courts of Heaven*). Ideally, the small group members will have received all of their resources prior to Week 1, but if not, ensure that the materials are present at the meeting and available for group members to pick up or purchase. It is advisable that you have several copies of the workbook and book available at the small group meeting, just in case people did not receive their copies at the designated time.

Call the meeting to order: This involves gathering everyone together in the appropriate place and clearly announcing that the meeting is getting ready to start.

Pray! Open every session in prayer, specifically addressing the topic that you will be covering in the upcoming meeting time. Invite the Presence of the Holy Spirit to come, move among the group members, minister to them individually, reveal Jesus, and stir greater hunger in each participant to experience *more* of God's power in their lives.

Introductions (10 Minutes—First Class Only)

While a time of formal introduction should only be done on the first week of the class/session, it is recommended that in subsequent meetings group members state their names when addressing a question, making a prayer request, giving a comment, etc., just to ensure everyone is familiar with names. You are also welcome to do a short icebreaker activity at this time.

Introduce yourself and allow each participant to briefly introduce him/herself. This should work fine for both small group and class environments. In a small group, you can go around the room and have each person introduce himself/herself one at a time. In a classroom setting, establish some type of flow and then have each person give a quick introduction (name, interesting factoid, etc.).

Discuss the schedule for the meetings. Provide participants an overview of what the next eight weeks will look like. If you plan to do any type of social activities, you might want to advertise this right up front, noting that while the curriculum runs for eight weeks, there will be a ninth session dedicated to fellowship and some type of fun activity.

Distribute materials to each participant. Briefly orient the participants to the book and workbook, explaining the 10–15 minute time commitment for every day (Monday through Friday). Encourage each person to engage fully in this journey—they will get out of it only as much as they invest. The purpose for the daily reinforcement activities is *not* to add busy work to their lives. This is actually a way to cultivate a habit of Bible study and daily time renewing their minds, starting with just 10–15 minutes a day. Morning, evening, afternoon—*when* does not matter. The key is making the decision to engage.

WORSHIP
(15 MINUTES—OPTIONAL FOR THE FIRST MEETING)

Fifteen minutes is a solid time for a worship segment. That said, it all depends upon the culture of your group. If everyone is okay with doing 30 minutes of praise and worship, by all means, go for it!

For this particular curriculum, a worship segment is highly recommended, as true and lasting transformation happens as we continually encounter God's presence.

If a group chooses to do a worship segment, usually they decide to begin on the second week. It often takes an introductory meeting for everyone to become acquainted with one another, and comfortable with their surroundings before they open up together in worship.

On the other hand, if the group members are already comfortable with one another and they are ready to launch immediately into a time of worship, they should definitely begin on the first meeting.

While it has been unusual for Sunday school/church classes to have a time of worship during their sessions, it is actually a powerful way to prepare participants to receive the truth being shared in the *Unlocking Destinies from the Courts of Heaven* sessions. In addition, pre-service worship (if the class is being held prior to a Sunday morning worship experience) actually stirs hunger in the participants for greater encounters with God's presence, both corporately and congregationally.

If the class is held mid-week (or on a day where there is *no* church service going on), a praise and worship component is a wonderful way to refresh believers in God's Presence as they are given the privilege of coming together, mid-week, and corporately experiencing His Presence.

PRAYER/MINISTRY TIME
(5-15 MINUTES)

At this point, you will transition from either welcome or worship into a time of prayer.

Just like praise and worship, it is recommended that this initial time of prayer be five to ten minutes in length; but if the group is made up of people who do not mind praying longer, it should not be discouraged. The key is stewarding everyone's time well while maintaining focus on the most important things at hand.

Prayer should be navigated carefully, as there will always be people who use it as an opportunity to speak longer than necessary, vent about the circumstances in their lives, or potentially gossip about other people.

At the same time, there are real people carrying deep needs to the group and they need supernatural ministry. The prayer component is a time where group members will not just receive prayer, but also learn how to exercise Jesus' authority in their own lives and witness breakthrough in their circumstances.

This prayer time doubles as a ministry time, where believers are encouraged to flow in the gifts of the Holy Spirit. After the door is opened through worship, the atmosphere is typically charged with God's Presence. It is quite common for people to receive words of knowledge, words of wisdom, prophetic words, and for other manifestations of the Holy Spirit to take place in these times (see 1 Cor. 12). This is a safe environment for people to "practice" these gifts, take risks, etc. However, if there are individuals who demonstrate consistent disorder, are unceasingly distracting, have problems/issues that move beyond the scope of this particular curriculum (and appear to need specialized counseling), or have issues that veer more into the theological realm, it is best for you to refer these individuals to an appropriate leader in the church who can address these particular issues privately.

If you are such a leader, you can either point them to a different person, or you can encourage them to save their questions/comments and you will address them outside of the group context, as you do not want to distract from what God is doing in these vital moments together.

TRANSITION TIME

At this point, you will transition from prayer/ministry time to watching the *Unlocking Destinies from the Courts of Heaven* DVDs.

Group leaders/class teachers: It is recommended that you have the DVD in the player and are all ready to press "play" on the appropriate session.

VIDEO/TEACHING
(20-25 MINUTES)

During this time, group members will take notes in their participant workbooks. Encourage them to ask the Holy Spirit to highlight certain points that are especially applicable to their lives.

Prayers at the End of Sessions

At the end of certain video sessions, Robert Henderson will lead prayers that will help participants enter into greater levels of freedom, breakthrough and discovered destiny.

As the leader, be sensitive to what the Holy Spirit does during these important prayer times, as it may mean you take some time *before* the Discussion Questions and allow God to minister to people based on what they prayed.

DISCUSSION QUESTIONS
(20–30 MINUTES)

In the Leader's Guide there will be a number of questions to ask the group, most of which are in the workbook also. Some questions will be phrased so you can ask them directly, others may have instructions or suggestions for how you can guide the discussion. The sentences in bold are directions for you.

Some lessons will have more questions than others. Also, there might be some instances where you choose to cut out certain questions for the sake of time. This is entirely up to you, and in a circumstance where the Holy Spirit is moving and appears to be highlighting some questions more than others, flow in sync with the Holy Spirit. He will not steer you wrong!

Some of the questions will lead with a Scripture verse. To engage group members, you can ask for volunteers to read the Scripture verse(s). As you ask the question in the group setting, encourage more than one person to provide an answer. Usually, you will have some people who are way off in their responses, but you will also have those who provide *part* of the correct answer.

There is a very intentional flow in the order of questions. The questions will usually start out by addressing a problem, misconception, or false understanding, and are designed to take participants to a point of strategically addressing the problem, and then take appropriate action.

The problem with many curriculum studies is in the question/answer section. Participants may feel like the conversation was lively, the dialogue insightful, and that the meeting was an overall success; but when all is said and done, the question, *"What do I do next?"* is not sufficiently answered.

This is why every discussion time will be followed with an activation segment.

ACTIVATION
(10-15 MINUTES)

- Each activation segment should be five to ten minutes at the *minimum*, as this is the place where believers begin putting action to what they just learned.

- The activation segment will be custom-tailored for the session covered.

- Even though every group member might not be able to participate in the activation exercise, it gives them a visual for what it looks like to demonstrate the concept that they just studied.

*Note: due to the sensitive nature of some of what will be confronted in these sessions, especially during the prayer times, leaders need to use discernment and discretion on what specific exercises are executed as a group, and which ones are done individually and personally.

PLANS FOR THE NEXT WEEK
(2 MINUTES)

Remind group members about daily exercises in the workbook. Encourage everyone to participate fully in this journey in order to get the most out of it. The daily exercises should not take more than 15–20 minutes and they will make an ideal themed Bible study.

Be sure to let group members know if the meeting location will change or differ from week to week, or if there are any other relevant announcements to your group/class. Weekly e-mails, Facebook updates, and text messages are great tools to communicate with your group. If your church has a database tool that allows for communication between small group/class leaders and members, that is an effective avenue for interaction as well.

CLOSE IN PRAYER

This is a good opportunity to ask for a volunteer to conclude the meeting with prayer.

Session 1

THREE DIMENSIONS OF PRAYER: FATHER, FRIEND, AND JUDGE

It could be that unanswered prayers have nothing to do with the timing of God. It could be that a legal matter is causing resistance against us in the spirit realm; a legal issue is stopping God from answering our prayers.

Session 1 begins with the most important foundation for unlocking destinies from the courts of Heaven—recognizing the three dimensions of prayer. We know our Lord as our heavenly Father, and we know He is our Best Friend, but how well do you know Him as the Judge? By the time you finish this course, you will know Him intimately as the Judge—and how and why to approach Him in that capacity.

First, let's discuss the importance of prayer. Jesus taught about prayer throughout the Gospels. In Matthew and Mark, for instance, Jesus illustrates prayer in a variety of ways. At times, He would pray all night long, He would get up very early in the morning to pray, or He would go off by Himself to pray. In the book of John, principles of prayer are cited. But in the book of Luke in particular, Jesus painted word pictures of prayer so we would understand what was going on in the spirit realm when we pray.

One of the main shifts for me when I began to understand the courts of Heaven was my concept of the spirit realm. I used to think that the spirit realm was a battlefield. When I discovered that the conflict in the spirit realm is actually in the courtroom, I was surprised at first. It's true that in the spirit realm, we are in a conflict when we pray. But here's the issue—*where* is that conflict being played out? Conflict on a battlefield and conflict in a courtroom are two separate things. If I'm in a courtroom but I think I'm on a battlefield, I could be using the wrong protocol to accomplish the goal.

When people have been praying prayers for a long time and haven't seen an answer, they may think, *I must be doing something wrong. I must be displeasing to God. Maybe I don't have enough faith.* We start blaming unanswered prayer on ourselves or think that it's not the timing of God. All the while, life is falling apart. Marriages are being destroyed. There is financial ruin. People are dying prematurely, and yet many chalk it up to the timing of God. I think it's a crazy idea to think that evil, even irreversible bad things happen because it's not the time of God to answer my prayer.

It could be that it has nothing to do with the timing of God. It could be that a legal matter is causing resistance against us in the spirit realm; a legal issue is stopping God from answering our prayers.

To understand that premise, it is important to study the three dimensions of prayer Jesus taught in Luke 11 and Luke 18. The disciples came to Jesus in Luke 11:1-2 and asked Him, *"Lord, teach us to pray."* Day after day they were watching Him pray and wanted His advice. In response to their request, Jesus said, *"When you pray, say: 'Our Father in heaven, hallowed be Your name.'"*

His discussion of prayer certainly included the identity of God as *Father,* but it did not end there. In this session, you will discover how three different identities of God actually involve three different prayer strategies!

SUMMARY

To pray effectively, it's important to recognize how to interact with the One you are praying to—God. He is a Person, not a formula. As a result, believers must learn how to relate to the different personality expressions of God when it comes to interacting with Him in prayer.

In the Gospels, Jesus offers three dimensions of prayer by introducing us to three unique identities of God—each one corresponding to a different posture in prayer. He is identified as Father, Friend, and Judge.

This first session is an introduction to the foundational concept of operating in the courts of Heaven—recognizing God as Judge. You will better understand the distinct prayer approaches that you can take based on what personality of God you are relating to.

> **YOU MIGHT BE SEEING DELAY IN PRAYER BECAUSE SOMETHING *LEGAL* IS RESISTING YOU IN THE SPIRIT REALM.**

INTERACTIVE QUESTIONS

1. Explain why you might be experiencing resistance or delay in prayer? List some possible reasons.

2. Read Luke 11:1-2. Explain how you would approach God the *Father* in the place of prayer.

   "Lord, teach us to pray, as John also taught his disciples." So He said to them, "When you pray, say: Our Father in heaven, hallowed be Your name. Your kingdom come" (Luke 11:1-2).

3. What do the names *Abba* and *Father* reveal about the nature of God the Father? How are they unique?

   - Abba:

   - Father:

> **IF WE ONLY KNOW GOD AS ABBA, THAT WILL LEAD TO *LAWLESSNESS*. IF WE ONLY KNOW GOD AS FATHER, THAT WILL LEAD TO *LEGALISM*.**

4. Read Luke 11:5–8.

> *And He said to them, "Which of you shall have a friend, and go to him at midnight and say to him, 'Friend, lend me three loaves; for a friend of mine has come to me on his journey, and I have nothing to set before him'; and he will answer from within and say, 'Do not trouble me; the door is now shut, and my children are with me in bed; I cannot rise and give to you'? I say to you, though he will not rise and give to him because he is his friend, yet because of his persistence he will rise and give him as many as he needs* (Luke 11:5–8).

When you approach God as *Friend*, describe what posture you are taking in the place of prayer.

_____

_____

_____

_____

_____

_____

_____

5. List some examples of friends of God in the Old Testament. How did these individuals specifically relate to God?

_____

_____

_____

_____

_____

_____

_____

_____

**FRIENDS ARE THOSE GOD CAN
SHARE HIS *SECRETS* WITH.**

---

6. When approach God as an intercessor, what is your prayer assignment? Explain how you think you should be praying.

_____

_____

_____

_____

_____

_____

_____

_____

7. Discuss the following statement and its implications: "If judgment comes to a nation, it's because the government of God failed in its assignment."

   How is the assignment of the people of God directly connected to the future and destiny of nations?

_____

_____

_____

_____

_____

_____

8. Read Luke 18:1–8.

   This reveals a picture of God as Judge.

   Then He spoke a parable to them, that men always ought to pray and not lose heart, saying: "There was in a certain city a judge who did not fear God nor regard man. Now there was a widow in that city; and she came to him, saying, 'Get justice for me from my adversary.' And he would not for a while; but afterward he said within himself, 'Though I do not fear God nor regard man, yet because this widow troubles me I will avenge her, lest by her continual coming she weary me.'"

Then the Lord said, "Hear what the unjust judge said. And shall God not avenge His own elect who cry out day and night to Him, though He bears long with them? I tell you that He will avenge them speedily" (Luke 18:1–8).

At this point, discuss what each of the identities of God that Jesus introduces reveals about how you approach God in prayer.

- Father: Luke 11:1-2

- Friend: Luke 11:5–8

- Judge: Luke 18:1–9

9. Why/when would you approach God as Judge?

ACTIVATION EXERCISE

Following this session, take some time to interact with God in prayer. It is essential that these sessions provide a spiritual laboratory where you can actually experiment with these new concepts.

1. Make a list of prayer requests. If you are in a group setting, encourage each person to make a list of the different things they are praying for themselves, for others, etc. *Space is provided for you in this interactive manual to write down your current list of Prayer Needs.*

2. After a few minutes, break up the prayer requests into categories based on the Father, Friend, Judge model. Space is provided where you can list different prayer needs under the three identities of God—Father, Friend, and Judge.

The goal is learning how different requests call for different prayer strategies. Based on what you learned about relating with God your Father, God your Friend, and God your Judge, categorize your prayer requests.

Most likely, you will be most comfortable with identifying your personal needs (God the Father) and needs of others (God your Friend). In future sessions, you will receive greater clarity on interacting with God the Judge, as this is where the courts of Heaven strategy will come into effect.

PRAYER NEEDS LIST

PRAYERS FOR PERSONAL NEEDS

GOD YOUR FATHER

PRAYERS FOR OTHERS/INTERCESSION

GOD YOUR FRIEND

PRAYERS DEALING WITH THE ADVERSARY

GOD YOUR JUDGE

Session 2

OPERATING IN THE COURTS OF HEAVEN

*It takes courtroom operation and courtroom activity to
be able to reach the destiny God has for you.*

Session 1 presented the foundational understanding of the three dimensions of prayer and how to move from not just seeking God as Father, not just as Friend, but also approaching Him as Judge in the judicial system of Heaven.

I've discovered that the ability to approach Him as Judge is critically important for breakthrough. God has for *every person* a destiny that's been prepared before the foundations of the earth, but here's the thing—it takes courtroom operation and courtroom activity to be able to reach the destiny God has for you.

Everywhere I go I hear frustration in the voices of God's people because they sense they were created and designed for something more than what they are currently. If you are shaking your head yes after reading that statement, that's normal. Most everyone thinks they could or should be accomplishing more. Maybe you're thinking, *I'm supposed to be having a greater impact at home, at church, at work....*

I have found that the key to "more" is to know how to go into the courts of Heaven and remove every legal thing in the spirit that the enemy is using to prevent you from becoming and accomplishing what God made you for. God is not resisting you. The enemy is blocking you from coming into the fullness of what God had in mind when He created you.

SUMMARY

Now that you have a basic understanding of the three postures of prayer—based on the three identities of God described by Jesus—you can focus more on the courtroom activity of Heaven, which involves God as the Righteous Judge.

When it comes to this courtroom language, many believers actually draw back in fear as the identity of God as Judge projects images of Judgment Day, condemnation, and guilt. The hesitancy Christians have in approaching God as Judge is due to a calculated effort of the enemy to undermine this essential identity of the Lord.

As a result, the adversary has done what he can to tarnish it because he fears you assuming this posture in prayer as it directly targets and dismantles his activity. Even though there will be a Judgment Day, the identity of God as Judge speaks of One who wishes to render verdicts on our behalf. This is the picture we must paint for ourselves if we are going to successfully operate in the courts of Heaven and dissolve curses that the adversary uses to detour and prevent destinies from coming to pass.

> **IN EVERY PICTURE JESUS PAINTED OF PRAYER,**
> **HE NEVER PUT PRAYER ONTO A BATTLEFIELD,**
> **BUT HE DID PUT IT INTO A COURTROOM.**

INTERACTIVE QUESTIONS

1. Explain the essential difference between the "battlefield" and "courtroom" postures in prayer. How can the battlefield approach actually be counterproductive?

_____

_____

_____

_____

_____

_____

_____

_____

_____

_____

2. Read 1 Peter 5:8.

> *Be sober, be vigilant; because your adversary the devil walks about like a roaring lion, seeking whom he may devour* (1 Peter 5:8).

Describe your understanding of how the devil, your adversary, devours people?

_____

_____

_____

_____

_____

_____

_____

_____

3. Explain how *sin* gives the devil legal right in your life. (Read and review Psalm 32 and Psalm 51.)

_____

_____

_____

_____

_____

_____

_____

_____

4. Explain what *transgression* is and how it can give the devil legal right in your life.

_____

_____

_____

_____

_____

5. Explain your understanding of *iniquity* and how the devil can use iniquity to enter into your life—and even future generations.

_____

_____

_____

_____

_____

_____

_____

6. How does iniquity give the devil a legal right to tempt you in a specific area?

_____

_____

_____

_____

_____

_____

_____

_____

_____

_____

**ALMOST ALL *STRONGHOLDS* COME
FROM AN INIQUITOUS ROOT.**

7. What impact can iniquity have on your identity—the way you think about yourself?

_____

8. How can *not* dealing with iniquity prevent you from walking into your destiny?

9. How does the enemy use iniquity to try and build cases against you?

10. Explain how iniquity can actually be standing in the way of seeing prayers answered.

ACTIVATION EXERCISE

For this particular session, the activation is a very personal process that involves you prayerfully asking the Lord to reveal any sin, transgression, or iniquity that might be in your life.

Please know, the process of dealing with these issues should not be lengthy or drawn out. It's not works-based. It does not have to take several months, weeks, or even hours. The reason believers live with these issues destroying their lives is simply because they never resolve to confront them and deal with them.

In the following pages, it is recommended that you go through the following interactive process so you can identify areas of sin, transgression, and iniquity; pray through it; renounce it; and position yourself to step into your destiny in new dimensions that, perhaps, you have never experienced.

Remember, the devil is a legalist, and he is looking to use anything against you to restrain you from fulfilling your God-ordained purpose.

1. **Pray and ask the Holy Spirit to lead you into all truth.** Do *not* become introspective—intentionally trying to find everything wrong with your life through this process. This is the counterfeit of genuine conviction.

   God is a loving Father who takes us from glory to glory. If He were to reveal every single area of our lives that needed adjustment all at once, we would be overwhelmed and feel defeated. The adversary will attempt to try and move you in this direction, so be vigilant and on guard during this process.

   - **Condemnation** comes from the devil and will always leave you feeling overwhelmed, overcome, and disempowered. The fruit of condemnation is hopelessness.

   - **Conviction** comes from the Spirit of God and is accompanied by the hope of victory. While the Holy Spirit will reveal to you areas of your life that are under the influence of darkness, He will come with the power and strategy to give you victory, thus filling you with hope.

2. **Ask the Lord to open the courts of Heaven for you.** We do not demand or command this—this is a privilege that God the Judge extends to us out of His mercy.

3. Now, ask the Holy Spirit to shine His light of conviction onto the following areas:

   a. **Sin:** areas where you have missed the mark.

   b. **Transgression:** areas where you stepped across a line; activity against God.

   c. **Iniquity:** sin that is in the bloodline.

4. For **sin and transgression,** simply repent for these things. Rather than providing a comprehensive list here, ask the Holy Spirit to convict you of these items so you can repent of them, turn away from these snares of the enemy, and take further steps toward fulfilling your destiny.

  a. Repent for areas where you have missed the mark of the Lord.

  b. Repent for areas where you did the right things for the *wrong reasons.*

  c. Repent for impure motives and thoughts.

  d. Repent for actions and deeds that are contrary to the will of God.

5. For **iniquity**—which is sin in the bloodline—you will need to deal with this slightly differently. In a future session, you will receive instruction on how to break and dissolve curses that have landed upon you and are hijacking your destiny.

   For right now, ask the Holy Spirit to start making these bloodline sins known to you. And remember, refuse to allow condemnation or fear to enter into this process. This is a sign that the enemy is trying to interfere because he is threatened by your freedom.

Session 3

YOUR BOOK OF DESTINY IN HEAVEN

The court was seated, and the books were opened.
—DANIEL 7:10

When the Bible says *the books are opened,* you need to understand there are all sorts of books in Heaven—the Book of Life for example. Whatever happens in the court will happen from the books, because the Bible says the court is seated and the books are opened. Why are the books open? Because many of the books are books of destiny.

SUMMARY

You will have clear vision of how to break off curses and iniquity in the bloodline when you understand that the enemy is warring against what's written in your book in Heaven. He knows that when you fulfill what's recorded in your book, the purposes of God will come to pass in the earth.

The following session will serve as an introductory study of Scripture describing the books of destiny written and recorded in Heaven. You will receive a Bible blueprint for what these books of destiny are and how what's written in these books is directly connected to the activity that takes place in the courts of Heaven.

Finally, you will receive an evaluation tool that will help you identify whether or not you are presently walking in your calling and destiny.

INTERACTIVE QUESTIONS

IT TAKES COURTROOM OPERATION AND ACTIVITY TO GET THE DESTINY THAT GOD HAS FOR US.
---

1. Read Daniel 7:10.

    A fiery stream issued and came forth from before Him. A thousand thousands ministered to Him; ten thousand times ten thousand stood before Him. The court was seated, and the books were opened (Daniel 7:10).

    Describe the language in this passage that points to "books in Heaven."

    _____

    _____

    _____

    _____

    _____

    _____

    _____

    _____

2. How does the court of Heaven render verdicts *with* human participation?

    _____

    _____

    _____

    _____

    _____

    _____

    _____

    _____

> ### THE COURT OF HEAVEN CANNOT RENDER VERDICTS WITHOUT HUMAN ACTIVITY AND PARTICIPATION.

3. Read Daniel 7:25–27.

   He shall speak pompous words against the Most High, shall persecute the saints of the Most High, and shall intend to change times and law. Then the saints shall be given into his hand for a time and times and half a time. But the court shall be seated, and they shall take away his dominion, to consume and destroy it forever. Then the kingdom and dominion, and the greatness of the kingdoms under the whole heaven, shall be given to the people, the saints of the Most High. His kingdom is an everlasting kingdom, and all dominions shall serve and obey Him (Daniel 7:25–27).

   How can verdicts from the court of Heaven bring you out of defeat and into victory?

   _____

   _____

   _____

   _____

   _____

   _____

   _____

4. Read Daniel 7:9-10.

   *I watched till thrones were put in place, and the Ancient of Days was seated; His garment was white as snow, and the hair of His head was like pure wool. His throne was a fiery flame, its wheels a burning fire; a fiery stream issued and came forth from before Him. A thousand thousands ministered to Him; ten thousand times ten thousand stood before Him. **The court was seated, and the books were opened*** (Daniel 7:9-10).

Describe the important connection between what happens in the court of Heaven and what is written in the books.

_____

_____

_____

_____

_____

_____

_____

_____

_____

_____

_____

> ## THERE WAS A BOOK IN HEAVEN WRITTEN
> ## ABOUT YOU BEFORE TIME BEGAN.

5. Read Psalm 139:16.

   Your eyes saw my substance, being yet unformed. And in Your book they all were written, the days fashioned for me, when as yet there were none of them (Psalm 139:16).

   How does this verse of Scripture describe the *books of destiny* in Heaven?

_____

_____

_____

_____

_____

_____

_____

6. How do you understand the following statement: Destiny is not something you create; destiny is something that you discover.

7. Read 2 Timothy 1:9.

   Who has saved us and called us with a holy calling, not according to our works, but according to His own purpose and grace which was given to us in Christ Jesus before time began (2 Timothy 1:9).

   What does it mean for your purpose to have "grace attached to it"? How does this *grace* indicate that you are walking in your calling and destiny?

8. How does the devil try to prevent God's purposes from coming to pass in the earth? How does this specifically relate to you and your unique book of destiny?

9. By what standard will we be judged for our lives on earth?

ACTIVATION EXERCISE:
INDICATORS THAT YOU'VE DISCOVERED YOUR PURPOSE AND ARE WALKING IN YOUR DESTINY

Take this time to personally evaluate if you are walking in your calling and destiny. When this is evaluation is conducted, usually a strong percentage of those in attendance raise their hands, indicating that they do not live with a clear sense of calling, purpose, or destiny. And these audiences consist of Spirit-filled believers!

Don't let the devil make you feel condemned about this! The truth is, the overwhelming majority of people on the earth live disconnected from their destinies—believers and unbelievers alike. When we live disconnected from destiny, unfortunately, it is easy for us to become landing places for the strategies of the adversary, which include iniquity, sin, and transgression. Curses in our lives and bloodlines continue to perpetuate this disconnection.

In addition, when we live disconnected from a clear sense of calling or purpose, we begin to live visionless lives, and where there is no vision people perish because they cast off restraint (see Prov. 29:18). When we live without a vision of what's written in our book of destiny, there will be no sense of order or structure to how we conduct ourselves.

On the contrary, when you have a glimpse of destiny you will live motivated to resist temptation and steward every moment of your life, driven by a clear sense of purpose.

Evaluation

The following are indicators that you've discovered your purpose. If you cannot answer these completely or have a difficult time with this exercise, this might be an indicator that you need to have your book of destiny opened. In future sessions, you will receive specific instruction on how to engage this process.

1. **You enjoy it...**because grace is attached to it.

   You can even *enjoy* a job or season in life that is not comfortable or favorable because, even though you're not in your ideal position vocationally, you live aware that God has you on the path of destiny.

   Do you enjoy what you're doing now?

Do you live with an overall sense of joy and fulfillment, or do you feel like everything is a fight?

Do you find peace in where you are right now, or do you live under the impression that the "next place" or "promotion" or "next season" will be what brings you fulfillment?

Do you experience an overall sense of purpose and destiny where you are, right now, or are you simply tolerating it?

2. **You will be good at it...**you will be graced with giftings and talents for what you're doing.

   Do you feel a particular gifting or talent for what you are doing right now?

   _____

   _____

   _____

   _____

   _____

   _____

   _____

   Regardless of your present place of employment or vocation, are there specific gifts and talents God has entrusted to you that you can use in your current position—right now?

   _____

   _____

   _____

   _____

   _____

   _____

   _____

   Take a brief inventory of some of the things you are involved with in life—activities, job, volunteering, etc. Which of these activities have unique grace on them?

   _____

   _____

   _____

   _____

   _____

   _____

   _____

   Finally, be very honest with yourself. Are there things you're presently involved with that you do **not** have a talent for, and yet you're doing them out of a sense of obligation? Perhaps you're doing them to be recognized or noticed? Perhaps you're doing them because you **think** you're good at them when, in fact, there are actually gifts and talents stored up within you that have grace on them.

UNLOCKING DESTINIES FROM THE COURTS OF HEAVEN *Leader's Guide*

_____
_____
_____
_____
_____
_____
_____
_____

Be honest in this process. Resist the enemy's condemnation, but do not be afraid of honest, self-evaluation. Where do you see God's grace upon your talent and giftings? This is, most likely, a clue to your destiny and calling!

3. **You will have success doing it…**because the grace attached to what you're doing will produce fruitfulness.

    Ask the Holy Spirit to show you the gifts and talents He has placed within you.

    Make a list of these, and then write some of the "success stories" that functioning in these talents has produced. You don't necessarily have to be overly spiritual when describing the "fruitfulness" that operating in your giftings has produced. Simply pay attention to the impact that these giftings have had on other people, the community, business, etc.

_____
_____
_____
_____
_____
_____
_____
_____
_____
_____

4. **You will be able to make money doing it…**because God wants you to make money doing what you're passionate about.

Would you honestly say that you are currently making money for what you are passionate about?

_____

_____

_____

_____

_____

_____

If you do not feel like what you are currently doing as a job intersects with your "passions," gifts, and talents, pause for a moment. Ask the Holy Spirit to show you how you can use your giftings in the place where you currently are.

Write down what He shares with you, as it is very important for the body of Christ to live motivated by a sense of destiny and assignment, even when they are doing jobs that do not appear to be "perfect."

_____

_____

_____

_____

_____

_____

Write down some of the dreams and goals you have and how these intersect with your gifts/talents. How would these dreams/goals coming to pass actually make you money?

_____

_____

_____

5. **The right people will bear witness to you...** because the grace of God is visible on your life.

Write down any confirmations or encouragements you have received from people indicating that you're walking in your assignment/destiny.

Pause and carefully consider this.

Prayerfully reflect upon words of encouragement, words of prophecy, and any other indicators you have received from people—both those close to you and maybe those who barely know you—that you are walking in divine destiny or that your destiny might be linked to something specific that needs to be unlocked. (Prophetic words will typically direct you toward something that might need to be unlocked for you to begin walking in your destiny).

Again, if you struggled answering these questions, it might indicate that you need to come before the court of Heaven and ask for your destiny to be unlocked and revealed. This is actually a good sign, because God wants to make this information known to you! You will be able to walk through this transformational process in an upcoming session.

This is not a process that will leave you with more answers than questions; if anything, it is purposed to confront the delay that seems to be restraining you from walking in a sense of fulfillment and purpose.

We will repeat this exercise at the conclusion of the interactive manual, as this is a very effective inventory tool for you to use on a reoccurring basis.

Session 4

WHAT'S WRITTEN IN YOUR BOOK OF DESTINY?

SUMMARY

The purposes of God being fulfilled are directly linked to His people fulfilling individual destinies. As what's written about in the books of Heaven comes to pass through the people of God, the purposes of God are advanced, the Kingdom of God is established, and the reign of God is released.

God's will shall be accomplished in the world, one way or the other. However, He has established an authority structure in the earth realm that involves human participation with divine purposes.

In this session, you will discover how to discern what's recorded in your book of destiny, specifically using Jesus as the key example. Even though Jesus was, is, and forever will be the eternal Son of God, He also took on the identity of *Son of Man*. He did this to perfectly identify with human beings, providing all believers a repeatable example to follow in their everyday lives.

INTERACTIVE QUESTIONS

1. Describe your understanding of how the devil can postpone the plans of God from being accomplished on earth?

> **THE PURPOSE OF GOD IN THE EARTH IS CONNECTED TO HIS PEOPLE FULFILLING THEIR DESTINY.**

2. What happens when the books of destiny are opened? What impact does this have on the spirit realm?

---

3. Explain how there is a case against you if you have a Kingdom purpose.

---

4. Read Psalm 40:6–8.

   Sacrifice and offering You did not desire; my ears You have opened. Burnt offering and sin offering You did not require. Then I said, "Behold, I come; in the scroll of the book it is written of me. I delight to do Your will, O my God, and Your law is within my heart" (Psalm 40:6–8).

   How do these passages in the Book of Psalms point to Jesus's book of destiny in Heaven?

_____

_____

_____

_____

_____

_____

5. Describe how you can use Psalm 40:6–8 as a blueprint for discerning what's in your book of destiny (because Jesus is your example).

_____

_____

_____

_____

_____

_____

6. Why is it important to develop a "prophetic ear" in order to access what's written in your book of destiny?

_____

_____

_____

_____

_____

7. Describe the relationship between prophecy and books of destiny.

_____

_____

_____

_____

_____

_____

_____

_____

8. Explain how what's written in your book of destiny is also written on your heart.

_____

_____

_____

_____

_____

_____

_____

_____

9. How does the ability to dream access what's written in your book of destiny?

_____

_____

_____

_____

_____

ACTIVATION EXERCISE:
TUNING IN TO THE PROPHETIC AND
RESTORING YOUR ABILITY TO DREAM

To access what is written in your book of destiny, there are two key areas that will help give you understanding—the prophetic and the ability to dream. Both of these are under significant attack, as they are instrumental in connecting people on earth to destinies that are recorded in the heavenly realms.

Both dreaming and the prophetic are bridges that connect people with a revelation of destiny.

In this activation exercise, I want you—using the very Scriptures that Jesus cited—to open your ears to hear the prophetic word of the Lord and also seek out what has been written in your heart.

1. *Tuning In to the Prophetic*

Sacrifice and offering You did not desire; my ears You have opened (Psalm 40:6).

Prayer:

Father, right now I ask You to open my ears to hear Your prophetic word. Right now, I come against any hindrance that is preventing me from hearing Your freshly spoken word. I recognize that it is Your will for all believers to prophesy and hear prophetically. This includes me!

Lord, I repent for giving my ear-gates and eye-gates to anything unclean.

I repent for dismissing Your voice speaking to me through signs, symbols, pictures, or unusual occurrences.

I repent for making declarations or confessions, actually saying things like, "I am not a prophet" or "I don't hear God that way" or "I don't have visions and dreams." On the basis of your Word, the very signs of Holy Spirit outpouring are the prophetic, dreams, and visions. These were not limited to a specific group of Christians—they are available to all who have received the Holy Spirit. I have the Holy Spirit, so I have access to the prophetic voice of God!

Open my eyes and ears that I might see and hear You, Lord!

2. *Restoring Your Ability to Dream*

I delight to do Your will, O my God, and Your law is within my heart (Psalm 40:8).

God, I recognize that Your law is written on the tablet of my heart. In fact, Your Word says that eternity is written on my heart.

Everything that You have purposed for me to do, to accomplish, and to fulfill has been written on the scroll of my heart.

I repent for embracing anything in my life that has hindered or even extinguished the ability to dream.

I repent for placing boundaries and barriers around my dreams, only conceiving of things that I can accomplish in my own ability or strength. Connect me, Holy Spirit, with the dreams that only Christ in me can bring to pass!

Even now, Holy Spirit, I ask You to release a fresh flow of dreams in the night and visions in the day. Help me to take the limitations off my imagination.

If I have been afraid of venturing into the realm of imagination, right now I place my imagination and dream life under the sanctifying influence of the Holy Spirit. Release me from any fear of dreaming, and I ask You to connect me with the very purposes You've written on my heart through the conduit of dreaming.

Session 5

RETRIEVING AND UNLOCKING YOUR BOOK

Until you have possession of your book of destiny and your book is opened so you can know what's in it, you cannot present cases in the courts of Heaven. Cases in the courts of Heaven have to be presented from revelation of what's recorded in your book. That's why Daniel 7:10 says *the court was seated and the books were opened.* What's going to take place in the courts of Heaven takes place based on what's in the books.

So here's the problem. Some people, even though there's a book about them in Heaven, do not have possession of their book. Some nations do not have possession of their books, some churches, and on and on. How can that be? Because someone in the family bloodline or something in the history of the country caused the book to be sold.

For example, Esau had a book in Heaven about him. He was the firstborn. He had an inheritance from God based on who he was. But guess what happened—he sold his book. When he was hungry he sold his book for a bowl of porridge. Then guess what happened—when he sold his book, he also sold his family's book, his family line, because he was a father of a nation. A whole family can lose its destiny because its book has been sold as a result of someone in the history of that family making an agreement with a satanic power that allowed it to take possession of that family's book.

SUMMARY

This is one of the most important sessions, as you will learn the process of how to retrieve and open your book of destiny. Up until this point, you have been receiving foundational instruction in the courts of Heaven prayer strategy and an introduction of books of destiny. Now, you will learn how to put these revelatory strategies into practice.

You will be introduced to two distinct processes for two groups of people. First, there are those who feel like they have no sense of destiny. For this group, they actually need to retrieve their book of destiny. Most often, the reason these individuals feel like they have no sense of destiny, purpose, or calling is because their books of destiny have been "sold out" through bloodline curses. Once the bloodline issues are dealt with, books can be retrieved.

Second, there are those who live with a vague sense of destiny, but there is no clarity on what it is or how it should be expressed. In illustrated form, it's like they have access to their books of destiny, but the books remain closed. The material in this session will also help participants learn how to open and unlock what's written in their books if they fall into this specific category.

INTERACTIVE QUESTIONS

1. How are you supposed to present cases in the court of Heaven? What serves as the foundation for your case?

_____

_____

_____

_____

> **PEOPLE DON'T HAVE ACCESS TO THEIR BOOK BECAUSE SOMETHING IN THE *BLOODLINE* SOLD THE BOOK OUT.**

2. Describe how "bloodline curses" can sell out our books of destiny.

_____

_____

_____

_____

_____

3. Explain the two indicators that reveal your family's book of destiny has been sold out.

    a.   You have no sense of destiny:

    b.   Sin in the family line:

4. What is the difference between retrieving your book and unlocking/opening your book?

5. Read Isaiah 29:10.

> *For the Lord has poured out on you the spirit of deep sleep, and has closed your eyes, namely, the prophets; and He has covered your heads, namely, the seers* (Isaiah 29:10).

Describe how prophetic revelation opens the books of Heaven.

6. Read Isaiah 29:11-12.

> *The whole vision has become to you like the words of a book that is sealed, which men deliver to one who is literate, saying, "Read this, please." And he says, "I cannot, for it is sealed." Then the book is delivered to one who is illiterate, saying, "Read this, please." And he says, "I am not literate"* (Isaiah 29:11-12).

Why is it important for books of destiny to be *open* in order for people and prophets to receive prophetic insight?

Articulate your understanding of the five principles to opening and unlocking your book of destiny.

7. Read Isaiah 29:13.

> *Therefore the Lord said: "Inasmuch as these people draw near with their mouths and honor Me with their lips, but have removed their hearts far from Me, and their fear toward Me is taught by the commandment of men* (Isaiah 29:13).

How is *true worship* important to opening the books of heaven? Describe what this might look like.

8. Read Revelation 22:10.

   And he said to me, "Do not seal the words of the prophecy of this book, for the time is at hand" (Revelation 22:10).

   How do open books of destiny and increased prophetic revelation confirm that a shift has taken place in *timing*?

HEAVEN CANNOT MOVE UNTIL BOOKS ARE OPEN.

---

9. Explain how tears of *intercession* can open the books of Heaven.

> **THE GOVERNMENTAL ROAR OF THE LION ALWAYS COMES OUT OF THE BROKENNESS OF THE LAMB.**

10. How is the *correct way* to approach the courts of Heaven? On what basis do you approach the courts? Explain why this is so important and how it will shift the way you pray.

_____

_____

_____

_____

_____

_____

_____

_____

_____

_____

_____

_____

ACTIVATION EXERCISE 1: RETRIEVING YOUR BOOK OF DESTINY

1.   **Evaluate:** The first thing you must do is evaluate which category you fall under. It is possible that your book (or your family's book) of destiny has been sold out because something in the *bloodline* sold it out.

2.   **Ask yourself these essential questions...**and remember, you are the only one who will be reviewing this material. You must be as honest and transparent as possible.

     a.   *Do I have a sense of destiny?* If you do *not* feel like you have any sense of destiny, purpose, or meaning, it is very possible that, due to some kind of iniquity inherited through the bloodline, your book of destiny has been sold out and needs to be retrieved. This leads to the next question.

     b.   *Does my family line have a history of multiple expressions of sin—immorality, addiction, debauchery, etc.?* Prayerfully evaluate your family's history and consider any kind of recurring cases of sin and immorality that seem to be transferred from one generation to the next. This might require further investigation, but simply begin with asking the Holy Spirit to reveal any of these items to you. He does *not* want you to remain disconnected from your destiny because of any kind of generational, bloodline iniquity. Trust that He will reveal areas that need to be addressed and repented for.

3.   **Repent, renounce, and break agreement!** As the Holy Spirit reveals areas of bloodline iniquity that need to be confronted, feel free to list those below and, by name, break agreement with them through repentance and renunciation.

Father, I come before You right now to confront the bloodline iniquities and sins that have been passed down generationally. Right now, I declare I am covered by the blood of Jesus. I declare that the blood of Jesus has made complete atonement, not only for my sins, but for the sin and bloodline iniquity I am going to list right now.

I repent and renounce... (list the specific areas that the Holy Spirit makes known to you).

_____

_____

_____

_____

_____

_____

_____

_____

_____

_____

_____

_____

_____

_____

_____

_____

_____

_____

_____

_____

_____

_____

_____

_____

_____

_____

_____

_____

_____

_____

_____

It's important to keep this written record, not to remind yourself of past sins or generational iniquities, but to remind the devil that repentance has been made for these items.

ACTIVATION EXERCISE 2: UNLOCKING AND OPENING YOUR BOOK OF DESTINY

Perhaps you are not dealing with some of the hindering bloodline issues. Maybe you even feel like your book of destiny has been made available to you but it remains closed and inaccessible. In other words, you have a sense of destiny and purpose, but it's elusive—almost like you cannot put your finger on what you have been called to do.

This is where you would come into the courts of Heaven and unlock your book of destiny. In the video curriculum sessions, Robert Henderson leads you in prayers that take you through the process of entering the courts of Heaven to access what is written in your book of destiny.

Throughout the coming week, put into practice the five principles that will help to open and unlock your book. Cultivate them in your life and ask the Holy Spirit to give you additional insight on how these items can help open books of destiny.

1. **True worship:** Cultivate a lifestyle of true, God-focused, Jesus-exalting worship.

2. **Timing:** Recognize and respond to the timing and seasons of God.

3. **Intercession:** Your prayers and intercessions have the ability to open books of Heaven over your life and also over other people, regions, and nations.

4. **Approaching the courts of Heaven on the right basis:** Remember, you approach the courts of Heaven on the basis of God's purposes, not on the basis of your needs.

5. **Apostolic decrees and authority:** When apostolic voices make decrees and release Kingdom authority, this has the ability to shift things in the spirit realm, thus opening the books in heaven.

Session 6

AN INTRODUCTION TO CURSES

One of the enemy's strategies against believers is to try and keep them from reaching and living their God-given destinies. He does this by presenting a legal case against them. That's what he sought to do with Peter, because if Peter lived his destiny he would push forward the purposes of God on a great level in a great way. It's the same way with us. If we fulfill our destiny in God, we will push the purposes of God forward and God's will shall be done on earth!

First Peter 5:8 says, *"Be sober, be vigilant; because your adversary the devil walks about like a roaring lion, seeking whom he may devour."* The evil one brings lawsuits and builds cases against us to have a legal right to devour us—our futures, purposes, anything he can possibly devour. Anytime I start sensing or feeling something like that coming against me, I try to figure out the legal issue that the enemy may be using to accomplish his fiendish plan.

This session is an introduction to the main strategy the adversary uses to find legal rights of entry into our lives and family lines—*curses*.

SUMMARY

Curses are what the adversary uses to prevent people from fulfilling destiny. Usually, the context of curses—generational and otherwise—deals with issues of the past and issues of the present. Past alignments, sins, or iniquities have introduced curses into family lines and have thus created a "present reality" filled with torment and oppression by the enemy. Likewise, curses are not just obtained through the bloodline but also through sinful agreements that provide the enemy open access to "land" curses on our lives. The higher demonic objective of curses is this: to prevent you from fulfilling your destiny.

The devil doesn't merely use curses to introduce torment or hardship into your life, although those are the immediate results. His greater goal is to use those curses to restrain you from fulfilling what's written in your book of destiny. Curses are directly aimed at what's written in your book.

In many circles, the subject of "curses" can be controversial. On one end of the extreme, there are theological perspectives that insist the redemptive work of Jesus completely dealt with the possibility of curses and thereby rendered it impossible for believers, cleansed by Jesus' blood and filled with the Spirit, to have curses "land" on them. There is validity in this perspective in that Jesus' atoning work on the cross completely and eternally broke the power of every curse. The other perspective, unfortunately, places an exaggerated emphasis on curses, to the point where everything and anything you might do, say, or participate in could open you up to be possibility of being cursed.

What is the Bible balance? In both the video session and through this interactive manual, you will discover how curses are very much a reality. Likewise, you will discover how the work of Jesus completely destroyed the power of every curse. The key to dissolving curses in your life is executing the verdict of the cross. While the cross rendered certain legal verdicts, these verdicts must be appropriated and executed by believers in order for the provisions of Calvary to be made manifest.

INTERACTIVE QUESTIONS

1. Read Proverbs 26:2.

   Like a flitting sparrow, like a flying swallow, so a curse without cause shall not alight (Proverbs 26:2).

   What does it mean for curses to "alight" or *land* on someone?

   _____

   _____

   _____

   _____

   Can curses just randomly land on *anyone*?

   _____

   _____

   _____

   _____

   _____

2. Read Galatians 3:13 and Revelation 22:3.

    Christ has redeemed us from the curse of the law, having become a curse for us (for it is written, "Cursed is everyone who hangs on a tree") (Galatians 3:13).

    And there shall be no more curse, but the throne of God and of the Lamb shall be in it, and His servants shall serve Him (Revelation 22:3).

    Explain your understanding, based on Scripture, of how people can receive curses even when Jesus *became* a curse for us through the cross.

    _____

    _____

    _____

    _____

    _____

    _____

THE WORK OF CHRIST MADE LEGAL *PROVISION* TO DEAL WITH CURSES.

---

3. Describe the legal transaction of the cross. What does it mean to execute the verdicts of the cross in your life?

    _____

    _____

    _____

    _____

    _____

4. What are some of the "verdicts" that the cross made available that need to be executed and appropriated by believers in order for them to be made manifest?

    _____

    _____

    _____

5. What are curses the result of?

6. Read Ezekiel 18:2-3.

    "What do you mean when you use this proverb concerning the land of Israel, saying: 'The fathers have eaten sour grapes, and the children's teeth are set on edge'? As I live," says the Lord God, "you shall no longer use this proverb in Israel" (Ezekiel 18:2-3).

    How does this Scripture reveal the *will and intent* of God concerning generational curses?

7. Read Ezekiel 18:30.

    "Therefore I will judge you, O house of Israel, every one according to his ways," says the Lord God. "Repent, and turn from all your transgressions, so that iniquity will not be your ruin" (Ezekiel 18:30).

Explain how this verse fits in the context of Ezekiel 18:2-3. Describe how it is possible for God to have a perfect will and intent that does *not* get fulfilled because of transgression (that opens doors for curses)?

_____

_____

_____

_____

_____

_____

_____

_____

_____

> **CURSES ARE THE RESULT OF THE ENEMY**
> **HAVING DISCOVERED A LEGAL RIGHT**
> **TO OPERATE AGAINST US.**

8. In reflection, discuss how it's possible for God to have a perfect will and intent—that people would live *without curses*—and yet people continue to open doors for curses to land upon their lives.

_____

_____

_____

_____

_____

_____

_____

_____

9. Read Numbers 22:6.

   Therefore please come at once, curse this people for me, for they are too mighty for me. Perhaps I shall be able to defeat them and drive them out of the land, for I know that he whom you bless is blessed, and he whom you curse is cursed (Numbers 22:6)

   What is one of the key purposes of curses?

> **A LEGAL RIGHT IS WHAT GIVES A CURSE THE OPPORTUNITY TO LAND IN OUR LIVES.**

ACTIVATION EXERCISE: DEFINING THE CURSES THAT ARE AIMED AT YOUR DESTINY!

Due to the level of controversy and confusion surrounding curses, it's important for you to articulate what you believe, based on what Scripture says.

Using the manual and video sessions as a guide, look up the following Scripture passages about curses. You might have interacted with some of these already as you've worked through the interactive manual. In order for you to dissolve the curses aimed at your destiny, the first thing you need to have is a basic understanding what curses are and how they operate. Many believers remain disconnected from this reality due to imbalanced or negligent teaching on the subject matter.

Read the following Scriptures. Write down your observations and reflections in the space provided below:

Proverbs 26:2:

Galatians 3:13:

Revelation 22:3:

Ezekiel 18:2-3, 30:

Numbers 22:6:

Based on what you read in Scripture, and you have studied in this session, articulate your understanding of what curses are and how they operate:

_____

_____

_____

_____

_____

_____

_____

_____

_____

_____

_____

_____

_____

_____

_____

_____

_____

_____

_____

_____

_____

_____

_____

_____

_____

_____

Session 7

COMMON LANDING PLACES FOR CURSES: PART 1

Listed in the following two sessions are some common landing places for curses. Some of these places may be new to you; others may spur thoughts that will deepen your spiritual awareness.

SUMMARY

Curses cannot land upon people without a cause—a legal right that grants permission for the curse to find a resting place in our lives and family lines.

The following two sessions will take you through different ways curses can land and alight upon people's lives. This information is being shared for one purpose—to help dissolve the curses aimed at destiny. Every one of these "open doors" provides curses with access points into our lives and thus gives them legal right to "land" on us and, if not properly dealt with, future generations.

Most likely, the reason we are dealing with some of these curses to begin with is because of gateways that were established through previous generation. Remember, a curse cannot simply arbitrarily land on someone. It has to be granted a legal right.

In the following two sessions, you will learn about how curses are granted legal right to land on your life. Likewise, you will be armed in the activation exercises to break, cancel, and dissolve these curses so you can unlock your destiny from the courts of Heaven.

INTERACTIVE QUESTIONS

1. Read Genesis 9:5-6.

   Surely for your lifeblood I will demand a reckoning; from the hand of every beast I will require it, and from the hand of man. From the hand of every man's brother I will require the life of man. "Whoever sheds man's blood, by man his blood shall be shed; for in the image of God He made man" (Genesis 9:5-6).

   Describe your understanding of *innocent bloodshed*. How can this open a doorway for curses—even if you personally were not responsible for the bloodshed?

   _____

   _____

   _____

   _____

   _____

   _____

   _____

   _____

   _____

   _____

2. Read Genesis 3:17–19.

   Then to Adam He said, "Because you have heeded the voice of your wife, and have eaten from the tree of which I commanded you, saying, "You shall not eat of it": "Cursed is the ground for your sake; in toil you shall eat of it all the days of your life. Both thorns and thistles it shall bring forth for you, and you shall eat the herb of the field. In the sweat of your face you shall eat bread till you return to the ground, for out of it you were taken; for dust you are, and to dust you shall return" (Genesis 3:17–19).

   Explain how disobedience to the voice of God can open doors for curses? What were some of the results that Adam experienced due to his disobedience?

   _____

   _____

   _____

   _____

3. Read 2 Samuel 21:1.

    Now there was a famine in the days of David for three years, year after year; and David inquired of the Lord. And the Lord answered, "It is because of Saul and his bloodthirsty house, because he killed the Gibeonites" (2 Samuel 21:1).

    Explain how covenant-breaking can create a landing place for curses. How is 2 Samuel 21:1 an example of this?

4. What is one common evidence of covenant-breaking curses in our lives?

5. Read 2 Samuel 12:11–13, where the Lord renders judgment for David's sin with Bathsheba.

   "Thus says the Lord: 'Behold, I will raise up adversity against you from your own house; and I will take your wives before your eyes and give them to your neighbor, and he shall lie with your wives in the sight of this sun. For you did it secretly, but I will do this thing before all Israel, before the sun.'" So David said to Nathan, "I have sinned against the Lord." And Nathan said to David, "The Lord also has put away your sin; you shall not die" (2 Samuel 12:11–13).

   Based on this account, how did *two* areas—what David did with Bathsheba and to her husband, Uriah—open doors for distinct curses to land?

6. Read 2 Samuel 12:14.

   However, because by this deed you have given great occasion to the enemies of the Lord to blaspheme, the child also who is born to you shall surely die (2 Samuel 12:14).

   Explain your understanding of how God dealt with David's sexual sin with Bathsheba and how He dealt with David's sin of committing innocent bloodshed.

ACTIVATION EXERCISE: IDENTIFY CURSES THAT MAY HAVE LANDED UPON YOU: PART 1

As you work through these next two sessions, it is important that you enter this time of interaction with the Holy Spirit very intentionally.

1. Ask the Holy Spirit to lead you through the process of identifying curses that might have landed upon your life.

2. Invite the Holy Spirit to protect you from condemnation from the enemy, as this tends to shut down the process of people evaluating possible open doors to curses. (They give up because they are overwhelmed by the accuser's condemnation.)

3. Refuse the temptation for intense introspection. Only focus on what the Holy Spirit reveals and highlights to you. Remember, the reason God would make any of these curses known to you is *not* to make you feel bad about them but to give you the ability to repent for these things and renounce their tormenting influence over your life. God reveals curses to you because He wants to break their hold over you. He wants you to execute the judgment of the cross against these curses.

4. Begin to pray through the list. Reviewing the different classifications of curses that were introduced in this session, begin to pray through them and ask the Holy Spirit to highlight anything that needs to be addressed—in your life or as the result of previous generational iniquities.

Some sample prayers are being provided next to each category of curses, along with space to write down what the Holy Spirit reveals to you.

Innocent Bloodshed

Holy Spirit, shine Your freeing light of conviction on any area of my life/my history where innocent bloodshed has been committed.

Wait on the Lord and listen for what He says/reveals.

Write what He shares in the space below:

_____

_____

_____

_____

Father, I repent for and renounce any innocent bloodshed that has been committed through my family line (name, specifically, anything the Holy Spirit brings to your attention and call it out).

I execute the verdict of the cross over this right now in Jesus' Name in the place of prayer. I declare that Jesus became a curse on Calvary so I would not have to live under the torment and tyranny of curses in my life.

Right now, because of His blood and because of the legal verdicts rendered at the atonement, I ask that any curses that have landed upon my life because of innocent bloodshed be broken in the Name of Jesus. Thank You, Lord!

I rebuke and cancel any assignment of premature death in the name of Jesus!

Who the Son sets free is free indeed! I receive Your freedom, right now, and thank You that all the tormenting effects are broken. Thank You, Holy Spirit, that books of destiny are being retrieved and opened right now!

Disobedience to God's Voice

Holy Spirit, shine Your freeing light of conviction on any area of my life/my history where there has been a major act of disobedience committed to Your voice.

Wait on the Lord and listen for what He says/reveals.

Write what He shares in the space below:

Father, I repent for and renounce my disobedience to Your voice (name, specifically, anything the Holy Spirit brings to your attention and call it out).

I also repent for and renounce disobedience to Your voice committed by previous generations.

I execute the verdict of the cross over this right now in Jesus' Name in the place of prayer. I declare that Jesus became a curse on Calvary so I would not have to live under the torment and tyranny of curses in my life.

I reverse diminished return for my labor, in the Name of Jesus. Where there was lack, I declare increase because the curse has been reversed!

Right now, because of His blood and because of the legal verdicts rendered at the atonement, I ask that any curses that have landed upon my life because of disobedience to Your voice be broken in the Name of Jesus. Thank You, Lord!

Who the Son sets free is free indeed! I receive Your freedom, right now, and thank You that all of the tormenting effects are broken. Thank You, Holy Spirit, that books of destiny are being retrieved and opened right now!

Covenant Breaking

Holy Spirit, shine Your freeing light of conviction on any area of my life/my history where I have broken a covenant or others in my family history have broken covenants (perhaps one of the most significant is marriage/divorce).

Wait on the Lord and listen for what He says/reveals.

Write what He shares in the space below:

Father, I repent for and renounce any covenants that I have broken (name, specifically, anything the Holy Spirit brings to your attention and call it out).

I also repent for and renounce covenants broken by previous generations.

I execute the verdict of the cross over this right now in Jesus' Name in the place of prayer. I declare that Jesus became a curse on Calvary so I would not have to live under the torment and tyranny of curses in my life.

I repent for marriages that ended in divorce (either your own or those of previous family members). Thank You, Father, that You are the restorer of the breach. You make all things new, right now, and I ask for the work of the cross to cleanse my bloodline of the effects of broken covenants.

Right now, because of Jesus' blood and because of the legal verdicts rendered at the atonement, I ask that any curses that have landed upon my life because of broken covenants be broken in the Name of Jesus. Thank You, Lord!

Who the Son sets free is free indeed! I receive Your freedom, right now, and thank You that all of the tormenting effects are broken. Thank You, Holy Spirit, that books of destiny are being retrieved and opened right now!

Sexual Sin

Holy Spirit, shine Your freeing light of conviction on any area of my life/my history where I have participated in sexual sin or others in my family history have participated in sexual sin.

Wait on the Lord and listen for what He says/reveals.

Write what He shares in the space below:

Father, I repent for and renounce any sexual sins that I have committed directly (name, specifically, anything the Holy Spirit brings to your attention and call it out).

I also repent for and renounce sexual sins committed by previous generations (name, specifically, anything the Holy Spirit brings to your attention and call it out).

I execute the verdict of the cross over this right now in Jesus' Name in the place of prayer. I declare that Jesus became a curse on Calvary so I would not have to live under the torment and tyranny of curses in my life.

I repent for fornication—sexual sins that took place before marriage (premarital sex and sexual acts, pornography, sexual fantasy/imaginations, books, movies, etc.).

I repent for adultery—sexual sins that took place in my marriage (sexual affairs, emotional affairs, pornography, etc.).

I repent for sexual thoughts and words—fantasies, lustful imaginations, and crude joking/ conversation.

Right now, because of Jesus' blood and because of the legal verdicts rendered at the atonement, I ask that any curses that have landed upon my life because of sexual immorality and sexual sin be broken in the Name of Jesus. Thank You, Lord!

Who the Son sets free is free indeed! I receive Your freedom, right now, and thank You that all of the tormenting effects are broken. Thank You, Holy Spirit, that books of destiny are being retrieved and opened right now!

Session 8

COMMON LANDING PLACES
FOR CURSES: PART 2

The landing places for curses outlined in the previous session are much more overt and openly recognizable. They can often be easily observed in both our lives and in our family history—innocent bloodshed, sexual sin, disobedience to the voice of God, and breaking covenants.

In this session, you are going to study some of the more *covert* landing places for curses. Even though these are not as blatantly obvious as those previously listed in Session 7, they nevertheless provide equal legal right for curses to land in your life and family line.

SUMMARY

This session will continue to explore some common landing places for curses. Specifically, you will learn about returning evil for good, curses obtained through authority (abusive authority and rebellion to authority), and finally word curses—where they come from and how you can break them, as these are some of the most common curses that we receive and we release.

INTERACTIVE QUESTIONS

1. Read Proverbs 17:13.

    Whoever rewards evil for good, evil will not depart from his house (Proverbs 17:13).

    How can returning evil for good open doors for curses?

2. Read Micah 2:1–3.

    Woe to those who devise iniquity, and work out evil on their beds! At morning light they practice it, because it is in the power of their hand. They covet fields and take them by violence, also houses, and seize them. So they oppress a man and his house, a man and his inheritance. Therefore thus says the Lord: "Behold, against this family I am devising disaster, from which you cannot remove your necks; nor shall you walk haughtily, for this is an evil time" (Micah 2:1–3).

    How can abusive authority open doors for curses?

3. Read Romans 13:2.

    Therefore whoever resists the authority resists the ordinance of God, and those who resist will bring judgment on themselves (Romans 13:2).

    How does Paul connect rebellion to judgment/curses?

WHEREVER THERE'S HONOR, THERE'S LIFE.

---

4. Explain what you understand *word curses* to be and how they operate.

5. Define the two realms of word curses:

    a.   Curses that come from the authority you're directly under.

_____

_____

_____

_____

_____

_____

b.   Curses that come from those in place of spiritual authority (but they are not your direct spiritual authority).

_____

_____

_____

_____

_____

_____

_____

_____

_____

_____

CURSES DON'T STOP UNTIL YOU MAKE THEM STOP.

6. Describe the process of breaking word curses over your life.

_____

_____

_____

_____

7. Discussion. What are some ways that you can protect yourself from *speaking* word curses over other people?

8. Discussion. What are some ways that you can protect yourself from *receiving* word curses from other people?

ACTIVATION EXERCISE: IDENTIFY CURSES THAT MAY HAVE LANDED UPON YOU: PART 2

As you work through this final session on identifying curses, it is important that you enter this time of interaction with the Holy Spirit very intentionally.

1. Ask the Holy Spirit to lead you through the process of identifying curses that might have landed upon your life.

2. Invite the Holy Spirit to protect you from condemnation from the enemy, as this tends to shut down the process of people evaluating possible open doors to curses. (They give up because they are overwhelmed by the accuser's condemnation.)

3. Refuse the temptation for intense introspection. Only focus on what the Holy Spirit reveals and highlights to you. Remember, the reason God would make any of these curses known to you is *not* to make you feel bad about them but to give you the ability to repent for these things and renounce their tormenting influence over your life. God reveals curses to you because He wants to break their hold over you. He wants you to execute the judgment of the cross against these curses.

4. Begin to pray through the list. Reviewing the different classifications of curses that were introduced in this session, begin to pray through them and ask the Holy Spirit to highlight anything that needs to be addressed—in your life or as the result of previous generational iniquities.

Some sample prayers are being provided next to each category of curses, along with space to write down what the Holy Spirit reveals to you.

RETURNING EVIL FOR GOOD

Holy Spirit, shine Your freeing light of conviction on any area of my life/my history where evil has been returned for good.

Wait on the Lord and listen for what He says/reveals.

Write what He shares in the space below:

_____

_____

_____

_____

Father, I repent for and renounce any evil that has been returned for good that has been committed through my family line (name, specifically, anything the Holy Spirit brings to your attention and call it out).

I execute the verdict of the cross over this right now in Jesus' Name in the place of prayer. I declare that Jesus became a curse on Calvary so I would not have to live under the torment and tyranny of curses in my life.

Right now, because of His blood and because of the legal verdicts rendered at the atonement, I ask that any curses that have landed upon my life because of returning evil for good be broken in the Name of Jesus. Thank You, Lord!

Who the Son sets free is free indeed! I receive Your freedom, right now, and thank You that all the tormenting effects are broken. Thank You, Holy Spirit, that books of destiny are being retrieved and opened right now!

ABUSING AUTHORITY

Holy Spirit, shine Your freeing light of conviction on any area of my life/my history where I have used authority to abuse others.

Wait on the Lord and listen for what He says/reveals.

Write what He shares in the space below:

_____
_____
_____
_____
_____
_____
_____

Father, I repent for and renounce any abuse of authority that has been committed through my family line (name, specifically, anything the Holy Spirit brings to your attention and call it out).

I execute the verdict of the cross over this right now in Jesus' Name in the place of prayer. I declare that Jesus became a curse on Calvary so I would not have to live under the torment and tyranny of curses in my life.

I repent for using authority to manipulate others to do what I want them to do.

I repent for using authority to control others.

I repent for using authority to spiritually manipulate other people.

I repent for the sin of witchcraft that is authority abuse.

I renounce the controlling spirit of Jezebel and break its hold over my life and previous generations.

Right now, because of His blood and because of the legal verdicts rendered at the atonement, I ask that any curses that have landed upon my life because of abuse of authority be broken in the Name of Jesus. Thank You, Lord!

Who the Son sets free is free indeed! I receive Your freedom, right now, and thank You that all the tormenting effects are broken. Thank You, Holy Spirit, that books of destiny are being retrieved and opened right now!

THE TRAUMA OF ABUSIVE AUTHORITY

Holy Spirit, shine Your freeing light of conviction on any area of my life/my history where I have experienced abuse by an authority figure (spiritual, teacher, parent, etc.). Thank You, Lord for desiring to break the power and effects of trauma in my life—trauma that opens doors to demonic torment.

Wait on the Lord and listen for what He says/reveals.

Write what He shares in the space below:

_____
_____
_____

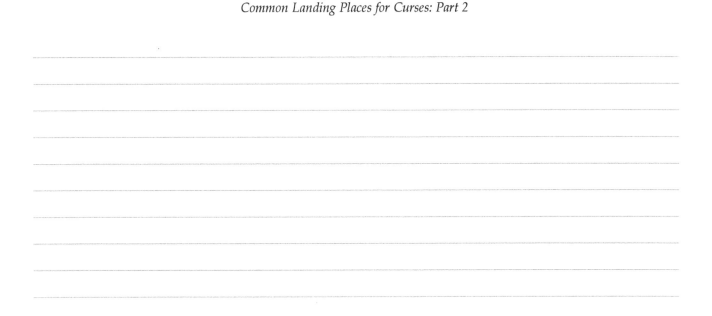

Father, I repent for and break off the effects of any abuse I have suffered because of authority figures in my life or abuse that previous generations have suffered at the hands of authority figures (name, specifically, anything the Holy Spirit brings to your attention and call it out).

I execute the verdict of the cross over this right now in Jesus' Name in the place of prayer. I declare that Jesus became a curse on Calvary so I would not have to live under the torment and tyranny of curses in my life.

I repent for unforgiveness and bitterness—my own and that harbored by previous generations.

I release my abusers now in the Name of Jesus. As an act of the will, empowered by the Holy Spirit, I set them free from my judgment and my unforgiveness.

I break off the effects of abuse and I rebuke the spirit of trauma in the name of Jesus.

I break off the effects that memories of abuse have caused in my life, which have given open doors to demonic torment.

Right now, because of His blood and because of the legal verdicts rendered at the atonement, I ask that any curses that have landed upon my life because of abuse be broken in the Name of Jesus. Thank You, Lord!

Who the Son sets free is free indeed! I receive Your freedom, right now, and thank You that all the tormenting effects are broken. Thank You, Holy Spirit, that books of destiny are being retrieved and opened right now!

Note: when receiving healing from the trauma produced by abusive authority, it is recommended that you prayerfully consider counseling to help undo effects of this abuse due to the severe and sensitive nature of this. Also, when going through the process of releasing forgiveness to others, it is recommended that you use John and Carol Arnott's book, *Grace and Forgiveness* as a resource (Toronto, ON: Catch the Fire Books, 2015).

NOT SUBMITTING TO AUTHORITY

Holy Spirit, shine Your freeing light of conviction on any area of my life/my history where I have not been submissive to authority (godly authority, governmental authority, parental authority, etc.)

Wait on the Lord and listen for what He says/reveals.

Write what He shares in the space below:

_____

_____

_____

_____

_____

_____

_____

_____

_____

_____

_____

Father, I repent for and renounce any resistance to godly authority that has been committed through my family line (name, specifically, anything the Holy Spirit brings to your attention and call it out).

I execute the verdict of the cross over this right now in Jesus' Name in the place of prayer. I declare that Jesus became a curse on Calvary so I would not have to live under the torment and tyranny of curses in my life.

I repent for rebelling against governmental authority.

I repent for rebelling against godly authority.

I repent for rebelling against parental authority.

I acknowledge that the spirit of rebellion is like the spirit of witchcraft, so I break its hold over me right now in the Name of Jesus.

In the place of prayer, I go into former generations and break alignment with past rebellion.

Rebellion stops here and now—it ends today. I repent for it. I renounce it. I break its power over me and future generation.

Right now, because of His blood and because of the legal verdicts rendered at the atonement, I ask that any curses that have landed upon my life because of rebellion be broken in the Name of Jesus. Thank You, Lord!

Who the Son sets free is free indeed! I receive Your freedom, right now, and thank You that all the tormenting effects are broken. Thank You, Holy Spirit, that books of destiny are being retrieved and opened right now!

BREAKING WORD CURSES

Holy Spirit, shine Your freeing light of conviction on any area of my life/my history where I have received or released word curses.

Wait on the Lord and listen for what He says/reveals.

Write what He shares in the space below.

Word curses you have received from others:

_____

_____

_____

_____

_____

_____

_____

_____

_____

_____

_____

Word curses you have released over others:

_____

_____

_____

_____

_____

_____

_____

_____

_____

_____

_____

_____

Father, I repent for and renounce any word curses that I have received or released (name, specifically, anything the Holy Spirit brings to your attention and call it out).

I execute the verdict of the cross over this right now in Jesus' Name in the place of prayer. I declare that Jesus became a curse on Calvary so I would not have to live under the torment and tyranny of curses in my life.

Right now, I undo every word curse that has been brought against me or that I have released over others.

1. I repent for every place where I have released a word curse over someone.

2. Father, I forgive those who have released word curses over me—or over my family/ previous generations.

3. *I speak off the word curses that have landed upon me.* Right now, declare the opposite of the curses that have been released over you. For every curse, declare the blessing of God. Declare reversal. Declare that what was placed upon you through a curse is broken through the power of blessing.

4. I declare that I let what's written in my book of destiny define me, not word curses from others.

Right now, because of His blood and because of the legal verdicts rendered at the atonement, I ask that any curses that have landed upon my life because of word curses be broken in the Name of Jesus. Thank You, Lord!

Who the Son sets free is free indeed! I receive Your freedom, right now, and thank You that all the tormenting effects are broken. Thank You, Holy Spirit, that books of destiny are being retrieved and opened right now!

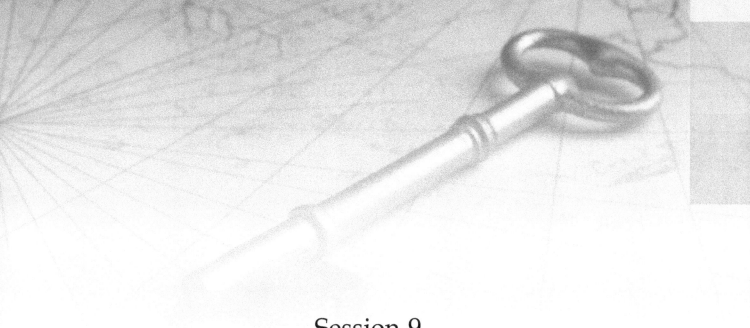

Session 9

UNLOCKING YOUR PROPHETIC SENSES IN THE COURTS OF HEAVEN

SUMMARY

In order to unlock what's written in your book of destiny, first you need to awaken your prophetic senses. It requires prophetic sight to visualize what is recorded in books of destiny, as it is a supernatural process. This is how prophets and those operating in the gift of prophecy make prophetic observations and declarations. They see glimpses of open books of destiny in the spirit realm and announce what they see.

By going through this concluding session, you will actually enter into the courts of Heaven and ask for prophetic senses to be unlocked.

To move in this realm, you need to recognize that Scripture confirms that all believers can operate in the prophetic. One of the results of the Spirit's outpouring, as outlined in Acts 2, is the prophetic operating in sons and daughters, men and women alike. While there are certain individuals assigned to be prophets in a five-fold ministry context, *all* believers have been given the ability to prophesy.

INTERACTIVE QUESTIONS

1. Explain the two essential components of entering the courts of Heaven.

   a. **Faith:** how do you use *faith* to operate in the courts of Heaven?

   _____

   _____

   _____

   _____

   _____

   _____

   _____

   _____

   _____

   _____

   _____

   _____

   **FAITH: LEARNING TO BELIEVE WHAT YOU SENSE
   AT LEAST AS MUCH AS WHAT YOU SEE.**

   b. **Functioning in the prophetic realm:** explain why the prophetic is so important to operating in the courts of Heaven.

   _____

   _____

   _____

   _____

   _____

   _____

_____

_____

_____

_____

_____

_____

_____

2. Read 1 Corinthians 14:1–5 in your Bible. Pay close attention to the following passages:

> *Pursue love, and desire spiritual gifts, but especially that you may prophesy. For he who speaks in a tongue does not speak to men but to God, for no one understands him; however, in the spirit he speaks mysteries. But he who prophesies speaks edification and exhortation and comfort to men. He who speaks in a tongue edifies himself, but he who prophesies edifies the church. I wish you all spoke with tongues, but even more that you prophesied* (1 Corinthians 14:1–5).

Based on what Paul is explaining to the Corinthian church, describe how it is possible for *all* believers to operate in the spiritual gift of prophecy.

_____

_____

_____

_____

_____

_____

_____

_____

_____

_____

_____

_____

_____

_____

WE NEED TO ASK FOR THE COURTS OF HEAVEN TO OPEN.
---

3. Describe your idea of what it looks like to enter the courts of Heaven. How would you go about doing this based on what you've read in the session/watched in the video?

_____

_____

_____

_____

_____

_____

_____

_____

_____

_____

_____

_____

_____

_____

_____

_____

_____

4. How can legalistic covenants prevent your prophetic senses from operating? Define what these covenants could look like.

_____

_____

_____

5. Read Revelation 19:10.

    And I fell at his feet to worship him. But he said to me, "See that you do not do that! I am your fellow servant, and of your brethren who have the testimony of Jesus. Worship God!" (Revelation 19:10)

    Based on what Robert shares in the video session, *who* is the person John tries to worship? How does this relate to you and your identity in the heavenly realm?

6. Explain why a *prophetic understanding* is important for you to enter the courts of Heaven.

> **A PROPHETIC UNDERSTANDING: WE HAVE TO READ FROM THE BOOKS OF HEAVEN SO WE CAN PRESENT CASES BEFORE THE COURTS OF HEAVEN.**

7. Explain the two agendas of the anti-Christ spirit:

   a. To deny and diminish who Jesus is:

b. To deny and diminish who you are in Christ:

A PROPHETIC RELEASE: AGREEMENT WITH THE TESTIMONY OF JESUS.

8. Read Revelation 19:10.

   For the testimony of Jesus is the spirit of prophecy (Revelation 19:10b).

   What does it look like for you to *prophesy* and release what Jesus is *testifying*?

_____
_____
_____
_____

9. Read Hebrews 12:22–24 and Ephesians 2:6.

    But you have come to Mount Zion and to the city of the living God, the heavenly Jerusalem, to an innumerable company of angels, to the general assembly and church of the firstborn who are registered in heaven, to God the Judge of all, to the spirits of just men made perfect, to Jesus the Mediator of the new covenant, and to the blood of sprinkling that speaks better things than that of Abel (Hebrews 12:22–24).

    And God raised us up with Christ and seated us with him in the heavenly realms in Christ Jesus (Ephesians 2:6 NIV).

    Describe how the description in Hebrews 12:22–24 gives you a spiritual picture of where you *are seated in Christ*—the heavenly realms.

    _____
    _____
    _____
    _____
    _____
    _____
    _____
    _____
    _____
    _____

10. How can you use this description to help visualize entering the courts of Heaven?

    _____
    _____
    _____
    _____

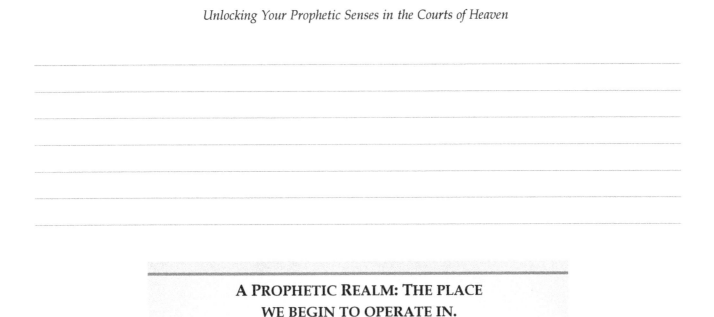

A PROPHETIC REALM: THE PLACE WE BEGIN TO OPERATE IN.

ACTIVATION EXERCISE: UNLOCKING YOUR PROPHETIC SENSES IN THE COURTS OF HEAVEN

To start seeing your open book of destiny, you need to have prophetic sight.

Follow the instructions provided by Robert Henderson in Session 9 of the video curriculum. At the conclusion of the session, he will lead you in a prayer that will help usher you into prophetic experiences in the courts of Heaven.

If you do not have immediate access to the video curriculum, you can begin to work through the daily entries and pray through the prayers supplied at the conclusion of this session.

ABOUT ROBERT HENDERSON

Robert Henderson is a global apostolic leader who operates in revelation and impartation. His teaching empowers the body of Christ to see the hidden truths of Scripture clearly and apply them for breakthrough results. Driven by a mandate to disciple nations through writing and speaking, Robert travels extensively around the globe, teaching on the apostolic, the Kingdom of God, the "Seven Mountains" and most notably, the Courts of Heaven. He has been married to Mary for over 38 years. They have six children and five grandchildren. Together they are enjoying life in beautiful Midlothian, TX.